In the Footsteps of Explorers

Lewis and Clark

Opening the American West

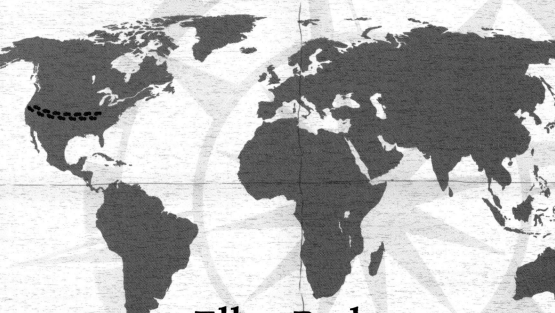

Ellen Rodger

Crabtree Publishing Company

www.crabtreebooks.com

Crabtree Publishing Company

www.crabtreebooks.com

For Mom, Dad, and Catherine, modern-day explorers.
"To find there but the road back home again"

Series editor: Carrie Gleason
Editors: Rachel Eagen, Adrianna Morganelli
Design and production coordinator: Rosie Gowsell
Cover design and production assistance: Samara Parent
Art direction: Rob MacGregor
Scanning technician: Arlene Arch-Wilson
Photo research: Allison Napier

Consultant: Jill C. Jackson, Director of Library and Education Services, Lewis and Clark Trail Heritage Foundation, Inc.

Photo Credits: The Art Archive/ Buffalo Bill Historical Center Cody Wyoming/ Mirielle Vautier: p. 19 (bottom); The Art Archive/ Chateau de Blerancourt/ Dagli Orti: p. 5; Bettmann/ Corbis: p. 8, p. 27; Richard A. Cooke/ Corbis: p. 30; Getty Images: p. 28; The Granger Collection, New York: cover, p. 11 (top); Rudi Holnsteiner: p. 13 (bottom), p. 29; Erich Lessing/ Art Resource, NY: p. 26; National Museum of American History Smithsonian Institution Behring Center: p. 13 (top); North Wind/ North Wind Picture Archives: p. 5 (bottom), p, 6, p. 7, p. 10, p. 11 (bottom), p. 15, pp. 16-17, p. 17 (right), pp. 20-21, p. 25, p. 31; Reunion des Musees Nationaux/ Art Resource, NY: pp. 8-9; Royal Geographical Society, London, UK/ Bridgeman Art Library: p. 19 (top); Stapleton Collection/ Corbis: p. 24; Other images from stock photo cd

Illustrations: Lauren Fast: p. 4 (both); Roman Goforth: p. 9, p. 18

Cartography: Jim Chernishenko: title page, p. 14

Cover: Sacagawea points Lewis and Clark west near the Three Forks of the Missouri River.

Title page: The Corps traveled 4,162 miles (6,700 km) from the Mississippi, up the Missouri, and across plains and mountains before they saw the Pacific Ocean.

Sidebar icon: An American bison, or buffalo. The Corps of Discovery was amazed by the huge number of buffalo that roamed the West.

Crabtree Publishing Company

www.crabtreebooks.com   1-800-387-7650

Cataloging-in-Publication Data
Rodger, Ellen.
    Lewis and Clark : opening the American West / written by Ellen Rodger.
    p. cm. -- (In the footsteps of explorers)
    Includes index.
    ISBN-13: 978-0-7787-2410-0 (rlb)
    ISBN-10: 0-7787-2410-7 (rlb)
    ISBN-13: 978-0-7787-2446-9 (pbk.)
    ISBN-10: 0-7787-2446-8 (pbk.)
  1. Lewis and Clark Expedition (1804-1806)--Juvenile literature. 2. West (U.S.)--Discovery and exploration--Juvenile literature. 3. West (U.S.)--Description and travel--Juvenile literature. 4. Lewis, Meriwether, 1774-1809--Juvenile literature. 5. Clark, William, 1770-1838--Juvenile literature. 6. Explorers--West (U.S.)--Biography--Juvenile literature. I. Title. II. Series.
    F592.7.R625 2005
    917.804'2--dc22
                                  2005001085
                                     LC

**Published in
the United States**
PMB 16A
350 Fifth Ave.
Suite 3308
New York, NY
10118

**Published
in Canada**
616 Welland Ave.
St. Catharines
Ontario, Canada
L2M 5V6

**Published in the
United Kingdom**
73 Lime Walk
Headington
Oxford
OX3 7AD
United Kingdom

**Published
in Australia**
386 Mt. Alexander Rd.
Ascot Vale (Melbourne)
VIC 3032

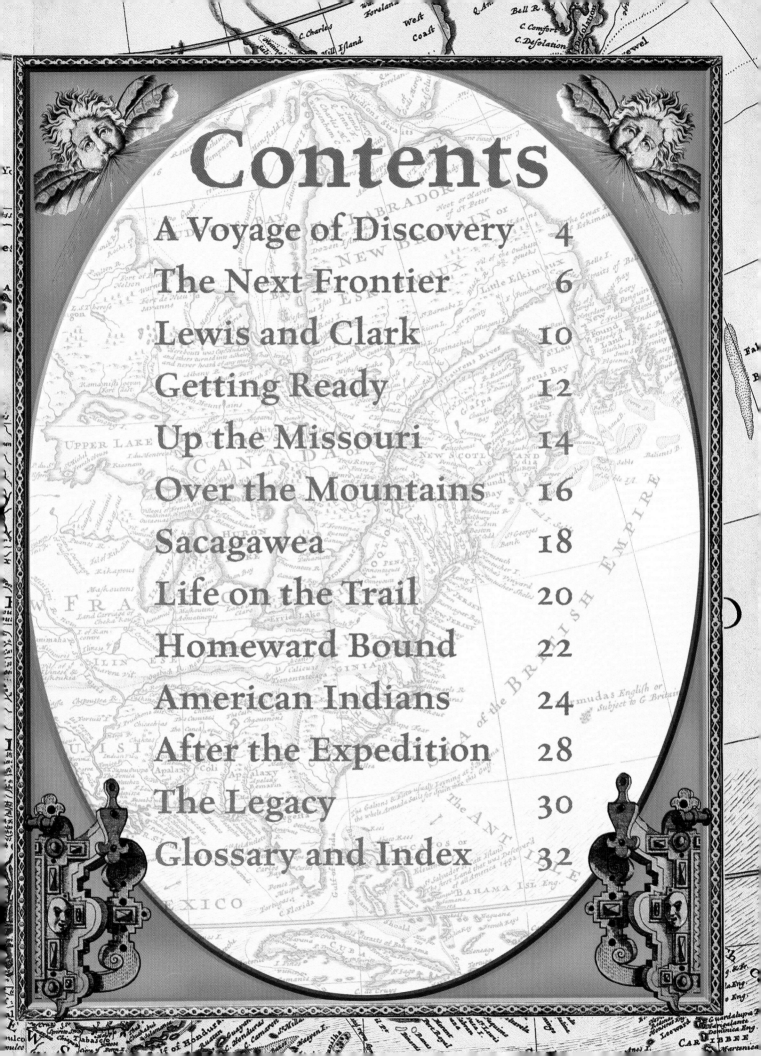

Contents

A Voyage of Discovery

Meriwether Lewis and William Clark were American-born explorers. They led a voyage of discovery through the American West from Missouri to the Pacific Ocean on the Oregon coast. Their dangerous journey charting the land, its people, plants, and animals, blazed a trail for the future growth of the United States.

Dreams of a Nation

In the summer of 1803, the United States of America was a collection of seventeen states clustered together from the Atlantic Ocean to the east and the Mississippi River to the west. Within ten years, the country's borders grew to include land as far as the Pacific Ocean and the Gulf of Mexico, due in part to the explorations of Lewis and Clark.

Lewis (right) and Clark (left) became the first American citizens to cross the Continental Divide and the Great Plains. They saw the Rocky Mountains and became the first Americans to reach the Pacific Ocean by land.

In the Words of...

Lewis and Clark kept careful journals that included information about the American Indians they met while traveling across the West, including how they were greeted, what foods they ate, their illnesses, and troubles. In this journal entry, Clark writes about meeting the Teton Sioux at Bad River, in present-day South Dakota.

> "... I was met by about 10 well Dressd. yound men who took me up in a roabe Highly a decrated and Set me Down by the Side of their Chief on a Dressed robe in a large Council House ... under this Shelter about 70 men Set forming a Circle in front of the Chiefs ... a large fire was near in which provisions were Cooking, in the Center about 400 wt. of excellent Buffalo Beif as a present for us ... "

(above) Without help from the American Indians they met, Lewis and Clark would never have made it to the Pacific Coast and back.

- May 1804 -

Sent by President Thomas Jefferson, (above) Meriwether Lewis and William Clark embark on an expedition through the West.

- November 1805 -

Lewis and Clark reach the Pacific Ocean.

- September 1806 -

The Corps of Discovery returns to St. Louis after more than two years in the western wilderness.

The Next Frontier

In the early 1800s, most Americans lived on plantations spread miles apart, in small farming or fishing villages, or in the bigger eastern cities of Boston, Philadelphia, and New York. The country's president, Thomas Jefferson, had immense curiosity about what lay in the West. He also wanted to protect the new American nation against foreign powers.

World Powers

When Jefferson became president in 1801, England, France, and Spain claimed parts of North America as their territories. All three nations had established **colonies** in North America and granted **trading companies** rights to the riches of the land. Those riches included fish, gold, and the fur taken from the pelts of animals that roamed freely in the vast North American wilderness.

(below) This map from 1803 shows the territories that belonged to the United States, England, France, and Spain before Lewis and Clark's journeys.

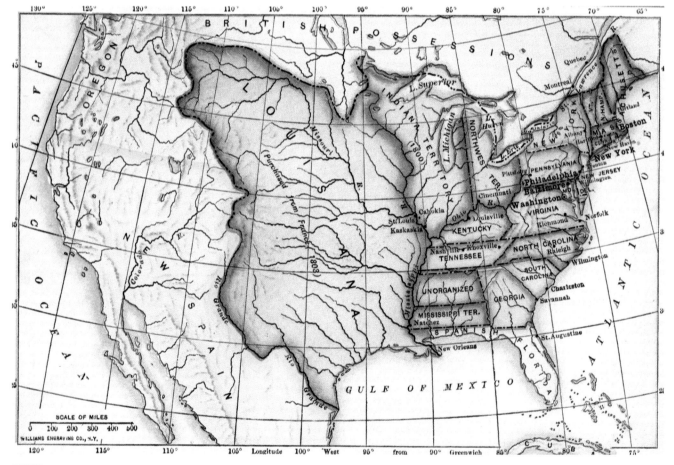

Imagining a Country

President Jefferson imagined that Americans would spread over the continent. Jefferson was a curious man who was interested in plants and animals. As a plantation owner, he understood the laws of trade. Jefferson felt that America needed more land where farmers could live and build prosperous lives for their families.

(background) The fur trade was an important industry in North America. Trading companies were set up to search for furs and to explore North America and claim land for England and France. The companies sent out many explorers who brought along voyageurs, French Canadians who paddled massive trade canoes. Voyageurs knew American Indian languages and cultures, and how to survive in the wilderness.

The Louisiana Purchase

The port of New Orleans was very important to the American economy. From the port, trade goods from other countries and from different states were shipped up the Mississippi River. President Jefferson sent James Monroe and Robert Livingston to Paris, France, to purchase a small tract of land on the lower Mississippi River, including the port of New Orleans. Monroe and Livingston were surprised when France offered to sell the entire Louisiana Territory. The Louisiana Purchase doubled the size of America and was the first step in the country's expansion.

Outside Threat

Jefferson also felt outside pressure to expand his country's boundaries. The British in Canada broadened their search for a trade passage to the Pacific and Asia. Jefferson knew it was only a matter of time before the British claimed the rest of North America as their territory.

Myths of Beyond

Few Americans knew what existed beyond the Mississippi River. French and British fur traders **plied** the rivers and streams of the interior up to present-day North Dakota. The area beyond that was a mystery. Some common beliefs were that the interior was home to woolly mammoths and mountains of salt. Some also thought that the Rocky Mountains could be easily crossed.

(above) A picture of the original treaty for the purchase of the Louisiana Territory.

(background) The map of North America changed when France sold all 800,000 square miles (two million square kilometers) of the Louisiana Territory to the United States for fifteen million dollars. In this illustration of the port of New Orleans in 1803, the French flag is lowered and replaced with the American flag.

The Northwest Passage

Fur trading companies in North America paid for expeditions across the continent, looking for a Northwest Passage, or an all-water route to the Pacific Ocean. Instead, each expedition found and claimed new territory. When Lewis and Clark set out, it had been proven that the passage did not exist in British territory to the north or Spanish territory to the south. President Jefferson instructed Lewis to find a water route across the continent that could be used for trade.

- 1792 to 1793 -

Explorer Alexander Mackenzie (above) leads a voyage through western Canada, about which he later publishes a book.

- March 1801 -

Thomas Jefferson elected president of the United States.

- April 1803 -

Louisiana Territory purchased from France.

Lewis and Clark

Before the Louisiana Purchase was even official, Jefferson planned an expedition to claim the Northwest. He chose his personal secretary, Meriwether Lewis, to lead it. Lewis spent a year learning and planning for the expedition.

The Woodsman

Meriwether Lewis was the son of a Virginia **planter**. His father was a **Revolutionary War** officer and a good friend of Jefferson. As a young man, Lewis served in the army, and was made an army captain. He later became Jefferson's private secretary. At Jefferson's plantation home of Monticello in 1802, the president and Lewis read a book that spurred on their desire to mount an exploration of the West. The book, a tale of explorations through the western half of Canada, was written by Alexander Mackenzie.

Letter to Clark

Lewis spent almost a year planning the expedition before he sent a letter to his friend William Clark, asking him to lead the expedition with him. Clark was born into a Virginia planter family and had fought in several battles with American Indians while in the **militia** in Ohio. He also served in the army with Lewis, and was his captain. Clark was a keen **marksman** and mapmaker. In his letter, Lewis told Clark that there was no other man on earth he would rather be co-captain with on such a dangerous and tiring journey. Clark wrote back that he would "cheerfully" join Lewis.

(left) Jefferson sent Lewis to Philadelphia to study with America's best scholars.

York

One person who did not join the expedition voluntarily was York, Clark's black slave. York was not even considered an official member of the Corps of Discovery. His skin color fascinated many of the American Indians that they met. Some American Indians darkened their skin with soot to protect them in battle and thought that a man whose black did not rub off must be very powerful. York became the first black man to cross the continent north of Mexico, and Lewis and Clark named a river and a group of islands after him.

Co-Captains

From the very beginning, Lewis and Clark shared command of the expedition. Most other expeditions had only one leader to whom a team reported. The Corps of Discovery members took orders from and reported to both captains. Lewis and Clark had learned how to work together when they served in the army. They each respected the others' abilities and trusted each other with their lives. Lewis did the early planning for the expedition and determined what tools to bring. Together, Lewis and Clark chose the men who would go with them.

(left) Clark's older brother, George Rogers Clark, was a hero of the Revolutionary War.

Getting Ready

To get the United States Congress to pay for the expedition, President Jefferson told them that the purpose of the voyage was to promote commerce. Jefferson also wrote Lewis a letter of general credit that said the United States would pay the expedition's passage back if they found a ship on the Pacific when they reached it.

To St. Louis

Lewis sailed up the Ohio River to what is now Clarksville, Indiana, and met Clark. The men sailed down the Mississippi River and spent the winter at Camp River Dubois, near St. Louis. Over the winter, the captains picked about two dozen men to join them on their expedition.

The Corps of Discovery

The men Lewis and Clark picked were seasoned woodsmen who had served in the army or worked as voyageurs in the fur trade. Some members had French fathers and Indian mothers and spoke French, English, and several Indian languages. Each man was inducted into the army for the expedition. They were expected to listen to and obey their co-captains.

(left) In his journal, Lewis recorded a natural event that no longer happens - a migration of squirrels. Lewis saw so many squirrels heading south while on a boat on the Ohio River that he set his dog, Seaman, loose to catch some and ate them for supper.

A Keelboat

Lewis had a keelboat made in Pittsburgh for the expedition. A keelboat is a small sailing vessel made for traveling and carrying cargo on rivers. Keelboats can be sailed, rowed, or **poled** on a river. The keelboat used by the Corps of Discovery was 55 feet (seventeen meters) long and eight feet (two meters) wide. The Corps of Discovery also had two pirogues, or large dugout canoes, that were used in the fur trade. The pirogues used six to seven oars and were towed when not used.

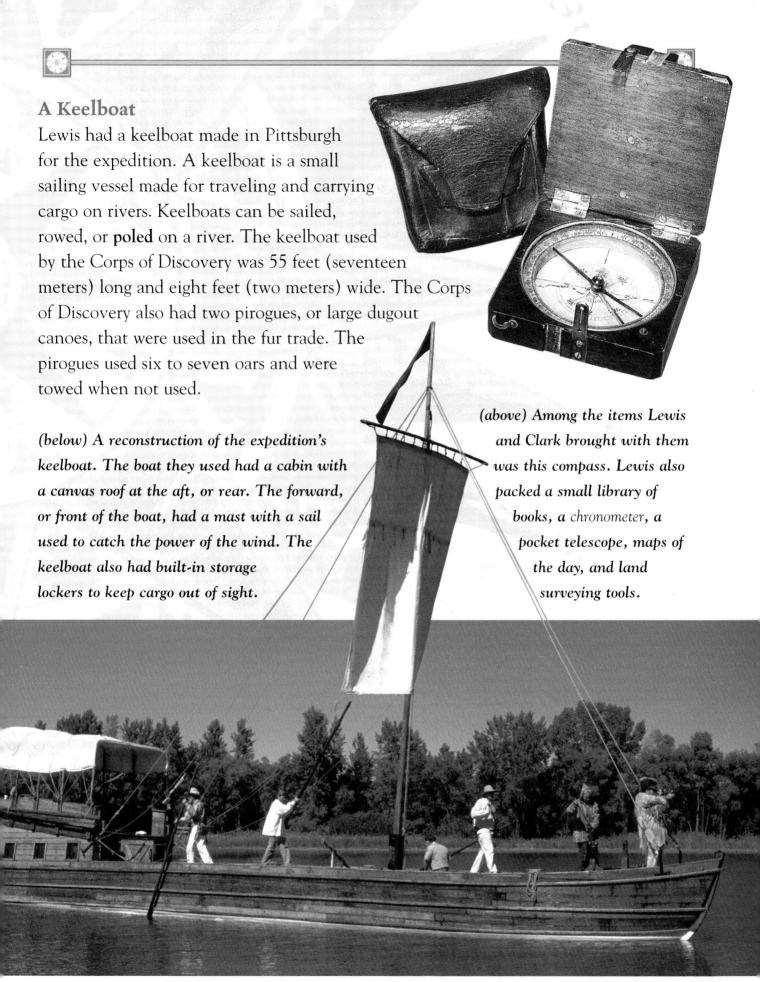

(below) A reconstruction of the expedition's keelboat. The boat they used had a cabin with a canvas roof at the aft, or rear. The forward, or front of the boat, had a mast with a sail used to catch the power of the wind. The keelboat also had built-in storage lockers to keep cargo out of sight.

(above) Among the items Lewis and Clark brought with them was this compass. Lewis also packed a small library of books, a chronometer, a pocket telescope, maps of the day, and land surveying tools.

Up the Missouri

Lewis, Clark, and the Corps of Discovery set out up the Missouri River on their keelboat, loaded with a mountain of supplies in May 1804. They expected to be gone for eighteen months to two years. They were headed farther west than any American before them. Their goal was to reach the Pacific Ocean.

Against the Current

The Corps of Discovery's journey took them through land as wide and flat as any man in the expedition had ever known. Lewis, Clark, and other members of the team noted everything in their journals. They poled and paddled steadily for weeks on the meandering Missouri River through the grasslands of present-day Illinois, Nebraska, Iowa, South Dakota, and North Dakota. Passage was slow as the men paddled against the **current**, making barely fifteen miles (24 kilometers) per day. At times, they had to use ropes to pull their boats.

Bitter Cold

The captains knew that they could not travel in winter, so they set up camp on the riverbank across from a Mandan village in what is now central North Dakota. The winter at Fort Mandan was bone-chillingly cold, but they survived it by trading with the Indians, who brought them dried corn in return for needles, scissors, knives, and other items. The Mandan also took some of the Corps on buffalo hunts. The Corps spent the winter making buffalo hide **moccasins** and beef jerky, and asking the Mandan questions about the territory upriver.

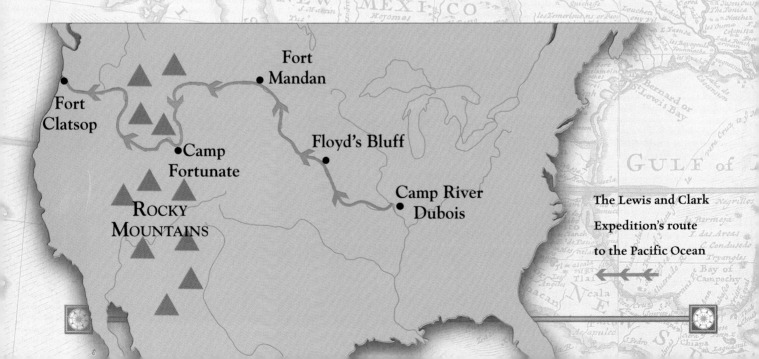

The Lewis and Clark Expedition's route to the Pacific Ocean

(above) A reconstruction of Fort Mandan. The fort they built included a number of buildings protected by a wooden stockade.

Westward Rivers

The Corps started up the Missouri River as soon as the spring thaw came, heading into country that was new to them. Grizzly bears tried to attack them several times on the banks of the river. They sometimes had to shoot the bears eight to twelve times to stop the attacks. The Mandan they met on the way told them that they would find a great waterfall on the Missouri and then mountains they would have to cross before finding the ocean. By summer, they had come to a fork in the river and could not determine which way to go, so they held a vote. Lewis and Clark wanted to follow the southern branch of the river and the rest of the Corps wanted to follow the northern branch. They split into two groups to explore. Lewis' group found the falls on the southern branch.

(left) Lewis and members of the Corps of Discovery spent days catching prairie dogs, which were later sent back alive to Jefferson.

- August 1804 -

Sergeant Charles Floyd dies from illness. The only Corps member to die on the journey.

- October 1804 -

The Corps reach Fort Mandan, their camp for the winter.

- November 1804 -

Toussaint Charbonneau is hired as an interpreter. His Shoshone wife, Sacagawea, also joins.

Over the Mountains

The Great Falls of Missouri proved a difficult passage for the Corps. Much to their surprise, there were five waterfalls. It took an eighteen-mile (29-kilometer) portage and an entire month to get around them. They were exhausted from the effort, and their feet were bloody from walking the jagged terrain in their moccasins.

Distant Mountains

The Corps feared spending the winter in the open air of what is today Montana. They could see the snow-covered tops of the mountains, but they were still weeks away from them. The Corps' goal was to find the Shoshone Indians and trade for horses that would carry them over the mountains. They had to cross the mountains before winter or they might die in the cold. They set up camp, hunted, and searched for the Shoshone for weeks.

A Chance Encounter

Just when the Corps began to lose hope, they came upon a group of women gathering roots. Amazingly, the chief of the Shoshone was Sacagawea's brother, Cameahwait. She helped them negotiate for horses to cross the mountains. The Corps called the place where they found the Shoshone Camp Fortunate.

Bitterroot Mountains

It took the Corps 22 days to cross the Bitterroot Mountains from present-day Montana into Idaho. The crossing was difficult and cold. The Corps could not hunt enough food and became weak from exhaustion and hunger. They were so desperate that they even ate their wax candles and one of their horses. When they came down from the mountains they met another group of American Indians, the Nez Perce, who fed the Corps salmon and berries. The Corps stayed with the Nez Perce for two weeks, building the canoes that would take them down to the Columbia and to the sea.

The Pacific Coast

The Corps followed the Clearwater River to the Snake River and then the Columbia, dodging boulders and rapids on the way. They were forced to make several portages, including around what Clark called the Great Shute, a rumbling waterfall on the Columbia. When they finally thought that they saw the Pacific Ocean, they were still 25 miles (sixteen kilometers) upstream on the Columbia. Stormy weather prevented them from reaching the **mouth** for another nine days.

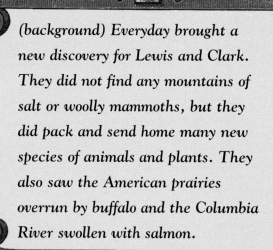

(background) Everyday brought a new discovery for Lewis and Clark. They did not find any mountains of salt or woolly mammoths, but they did pack and send home many new species of animals and plants. They also saw the American prairies overrun by buffalo and the Columbia River swollen with salmon.

(right) A pass through the Bitterroot Mountains on what is today the Lewis and Clark Trail. The Bitterroot Mountains were so steep that many of the Corps' horses lost their footing, fell backwards, and rolled down. The Corps lost their last thermometer when a horse fell on it.

Sacagawea

Sacagawea was about fifteen years old when she met Lewis and Clark. She was the wife of a fur trader who had been hired as an interpreter. Sacagawea had a baby boy shortly before the Corps left on their journey. She helped the expedition by translating.

Early Life

Sacagawea was captured at about age twelve in a Hidatsa raid on her Shoshone village in the Rocky Mountains, in present-day Idaho. The Hidatsa were enemies of her people. As a captive, she lived among the Hidatsa and Mandans, learning their language and customs. When she was about fourteen, Sacagawea and another woman were sold to Toussaint Charbonneau, who made them his wives.

Birth of a Son

During the winter the Corps spent at Fort Mandan, Lewis helped Sacagawea give birth to a son. The child was named Jean-Baptiste, but later given the nickname Pompey, or Pomp, by Clark. When the Captains hired Charbonneau as interpreter, on the condition he bring Sacagawea, their son became the Corps of Discovery's youngest member.

(above) Sacagawea's name meant Bird Woman. Clark relied on her knowledge of the land and called her his "pilot."

Peacekeeping

Sacagawea's presence among the Lewis and Clark Expedition helped convince many Indian tribes they met that the Corps was friendly, because war parties never traveled with women. She was also calm under pressure. Once, when Charbonneau nearly swamped a canoe they were in, her husband panicked but she did not, and saved the men's journals and supplies from the river.

(above) A painting of Sacagawea and Captain Lewis meeting the Shoshone.

Shoshone Reunion

When the Corps of Discovery sought out the Shoshone to buy horses to get them over the Rockies, Sacagawea experienced an amazing coincidence. She recognized the Shoshone chief, Cameahwait, as her brother. Crying with joy, she threw her blanket over him as a gesture of love. After a reunion with her people, Sacagawea left with her husband and the Corps.

(left) Carrying her baby on her back in a cradle board, Sacagawea did as much work as any man on the expedition.

(right) Sacagawea gathered wild roots, vegetables, and fruits to add to the Corps' diet of wild meat, such as buffalo and elk. Some of the plants American Indians used, such as the roots of the purple cornflower, or echinacea, were unknown to Lewis and Clark.

Life on the Trail

The survival of the Corps of Discovery depended upon many things, including meeting friendly Indian tribes and finding enough food to eat. Most importantly, their survival depended on teamwork.

Working Together

The early months of the expedition were filled with days of learning. The success of the journey depended upon working together and getting along. During the first few months, several men were fired or **court martialed** for not obeying orders, for fighting, or for talking back to Lewis and Clark. Over time, the Corps began to work together without fights, brawls, or drinking on the job.

Hunting and Gathering

Each member of the Corps brought different skills to their position. Some members, such as French fur trader George Drouillard, were excellent hunters. The Corps bought four horses from the Mandans, which were ridden by members who followed the boat along the river and ventured further to hunt during the day. Each member of the Corps ate up to nine pounds (four kilograms) of fresh meat per day. When supplies of wild game, such as deer, elk, or buffalo, were scarce, one thing they ate was dog. Corps members developed a taste for the animals and purchased them from American Indians.

(background) Lewis purchased 30 half barrels of flour, seven barrels of salt, beans, sugar, hog's lard, biscuits, as well as many barrels of corn meal, hulled corn, and dried peas and beans for the trip up the Missouri. Toussaint Charbonneau became the Corps' cook because he proved as skillful at making meals as translating.

(below) The Corps suffered from snake bites, mosquito and other insect bites, and illnesses, such as dysentery, and large boils.

Jerusalem Artichokes

Jerusalem artichokes are not artichokes, but the root of a plant. Lewis noted in his journal that Sacagawea dug "wild artichokes" when food ran low on the Great Plains and prepared them by cooking them over a fire.

What you need:
five to ten Jerusalem artichokes
2 tbsp (30 mL) melted butter
2 tbsp (30 mL) olive or cooking oil
salt and pepper

What to do:
Clean artichokes like potatoes and cut and quarter. Mix the melted butter with the oil. Add artichokes, salt, and pepper. Mix together. Spread artichokes into a low-sided pan (not aluminum). Bake at 350°F (175°C) for 30-60 minutes or until tender. Check frequently, as the artichokes will turn mushy if overcooked.

(top) Jerusalem artichokes are the root of a sunflower-like plant.

(above) One member of the Corps of Discovery, Pierre Cruzatte, was a good fiddle player. While at Fort Mandan, the Corps passed the long, lonely winter by holding occasional "jigs" where they entertained the Mandan with music and dances.

(right) To stop grizzly bear attacks, the Corps had to shoot them many times with their rifles, called flintlock rifles.

Homeward Bound

The Lewis and Clark Expedition's goal of reaching the Pacific Ocean from St. Louis took two years of grueling work. Once they saw the ocean, their minds were set on their return journey home.

Fort Clatsop

Lewis and Clark hoped to see a passing ship on the Pacific that would take them or a message home. When a ship did not come, the Corps of Discovery debated on which side of the river to build a fort. The Corps, including York and Sacagawea, voted and it was decided to build near what is today Astoria, Oregon. They settled in for another winter. At Fort Clatsop, they traded for food with the Clatsop and Chinook Indians.

Over the Mountains

Winter had barely ended when the Corps left Fort Clatsop. They headed back the way they came: up the Columbia River to the Nez Perce who had kept their horses for the winter, and over the Bitterroot Mountains again. Once over the Bitterroots, Lewis and Clark split the Corps into two groups to explore the area. They agreed to meet up where the Missouri and Yellowstone Rivers **confluence**.

(background) The Oregon coast has very wet winters. Most of the Corps spent the winter at Fort Clatsop hunting elk for food, trading with the coastal Indians, and sewing clothes for the trip home.

Down the Missouri and Home

Lewis' team took canoes and headed down the Missouri River. Clark and his men built two dugout canoes and traveled on the Yellowstone River. They met in present-day North Dakota near the Little Knife River and proceeded together to Fort Mandan. This time they traveled with the river's current. At Fort Mandan, the Corps dropped off Sacagawea, her husband, and her son. After paying their respects at the grave of Sergeant Floyd, at what is now Floyd's Bluff in Sioux City, Iowa, they headed for St. Louis. By September 1806, the boat began to meet other boats on their way up the Missouri. People back east had given up hope that any member of the Lewis and Clark Expedition had survived. When word spread that the boat was heading down river, an excited crowd gathered to cheer at the docks in St. Louis. Lewis wrote a letter to President Jefferson telling him that the Corps of Discovery had completed its mission.

(left) Lewis took three men and explored the Marias River, where they met a Blackfoot hunting party. They camped with the party but during the night a fight broke out and two Blackfoot were killed. Lewis's group rode hard and fast for 24 hours to meet up again with the rest of their group at the Missouri.

- March 1806 -

Leave Fort Clatsop.

- July 1806 -

Near Yellowstone, Clark carves his name into a rock, which he calls Pompey's tower.

- August 1806 -

Return to Mandan villages.

American Indians

Many American Indians of the West were accustomed to seeing fur traders come and go from their lands. The Lewis and Clark Expedition did not seem to be a threat because they traveled with a woman and a baby. It is believed that some American Indian groups avoided contact with them altogether.

Village Life

The journals kept by members of the expedition are a record of how some American Indians lived 200 years ago. The journals give descriptions of the kinds of houses they lived in, what they ate, wore, and how they got along with each other.

(below and right) From the journals, people now know that the Mandan were farmers and hunters. They grew corn, beans, squash, and tobacco.

Nomadic Inhabitants

At the time of the Lewis and Clark Expedition, many Plains Indians followed buffalo migration and did not live permanently in one place. The Great Plains were a fruitful hunting ground for buffalo, elk, bison, deer, and antelope. Buffalo was not only the major food, but also provided shelter and clothing. The Plains Indians made buffalo hide tepees with long poles that could easily be taken down and moved, along with all of their belongings. Women set the tepees up when a herd was spotted and the men hunted the animals using bows and arrows. Buffalo meat was eaten fresh and dried. Buffalo horns were carved into spoons and cups. The bones were made into weapons and the buffalo intestines were cleaned and used to carry water.

Coastal Indians

While the Plains Indians were dependent on the buffalo herds that roamed their lands, the American Indians closer to the Pacific Ocean were dependent on salmon. They even used the salmon skins for clothing. The Clatsop, Tilamook, and Chinook Indians lived in villages of large, permanent houses with towering totem poles. They built boats to ply the Columbia River and fish for salmon that they ate fresh, or dried for later use or trade. Some Pacific Coast Indians wore clothing made from tree bark, which they took from the massive trees that grew in the wet coastal forests.

(background) Some lower Columbia Indians were called the Flathead Indians by Lewis and Clark. They lived on the plains west of the Rocky Mountains. They were called the Flatheads because they used a board to apply pressure to the heads of children, which over time, flattened their heads. They believed this made their heads look beautiful.

Claiming the Land

Part of the mission of the Corps of Discovery was to meet the people who lived in the West, and claim their land for the United States. When they met a new group of American Indians, Lewis and Clark told them that they were members of a great nation with a president, or "father," who wanted to treat them well. They promised peace if the Indians were peaceful in return.

Trinkets, Trade, and Ceremonies

The Corps brought along many gifts and items to trade with the American Indians, including kettles, beads, and cloth. Lewis also had several peace medals made before the journey and he gave them to tribes they met. Some American Indians gave them food and horses when they most needed them and invited them to feasts and to celebrate with them. The friendship and kindness of Indians kept them from starving and being lost in the wilderness. Still, the Corps often feared for their lives meeting new American Indian tribes.

(left) An artifact from the Lewis and Clark Expedition. This wicker hat of the Nootka Indians was collected near the Columbia River.

Early Contact

War and alliances were common for the American Indians at this time. Fur traders had been making trading alliances with different Indian tribes for over 300 years. Often, Lewis and Clark found that the groups with the strongest trading alliances were the most powerful and the most unfriendly with them. The Teton Sioux were one such group. The Corps met the Teton Sioux, also called the Lakotas, in South Dakota. The Lakotas were a powerful nation who controlled the flow of trade on the Missouri River. They demanded that the Corps pay a toll to pass through their lands. When Lewis and Clark refused, the Lakotas tried to seize their boats. The two groups almost fought, but the issue was resolved peacefully.

(background) Sacagawea points the way for the Lewis and Clark Expedition. Accompanied by a woman and child, they were seen as less of a threat by Indians. Near the end of their expedition, they ran out of trade items and traded medical services and their own clothing. Sacagawea was even persuaded to give up a precious beaded belt so that Lewis could trade it for a Chinook chief's cape of sea otter fur.

After the Expedition

The Corps was welcomed back to St. Louis by a cheering crowd. So much time had passed that many people back home believed they were dead. Lewis and Clark were the guests of honor at many balls and banquets. People wanted to meet the men who had done what no other citizens of the United States had.

Disbanding the Corps

When they joined the Corps, the band of soldiers and woodsmen knew they would be making history. They did not bargain for the misery of three winters on the trek, almost starving to death, and the aching knowledge that they may never see their loved ones again. In the beginning, most of them were mostly concerned with their pay.

Into the Future

At the end of their three-year journey, the members of the Corps of Discovery, not including York, collected double pay and were awarded land in the country's new western territory. Few took advantage of the land, choosing instead to go back into the fur trade. Some were killed by American Indians when they ventured further into new territory. The last member of the Corps died an old man in the mid-1800s.

(left) The Lewis and Clark Expedition named many streams, rivers, and landforms that they passed. There are also many monuments to the members of the Corps of Discovery. Many landmarks, statues, lakes, and mountains are dedicated to Sacagawea.

(above) Today, many people like to reenact, or play out, the journey taken by Lewis and Clark. They do this to commemorate the explorers' voyage.

What Happened to Lewis and Clark?

After the expedition, President Jefferson made Lewis **governor** of Upper Louisiana. The journey to the West was Lewis' greatest adventure. After the expedition, he was unhappy, ill, and a failure as governor and in business. Lewis shot himself at an inn in Tennessee. Clark outlived his friend by several decades. After the expedition, he became governor of the new Missouri Territory and later **superintendent** of **Indian Affairs**. Clark married twice and had five children with his first wife and two more with his second wife. He also adopted several children, including Sacagawea's son and daughter.

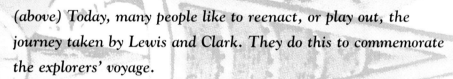

- October 1809 -

Meriwether Lewis dies at age 35.

- 1812 -

Sacagawea is believed to have died of a fever at age 25.

- September 1838 -

Clark dies at the age of 69.

The Legacy

The journey of the Corps of Discovery has become an American epic. The group of 33 found a wide and varied land which they claimed for the United States. Their journey changed the country, the continent, and its peoples forever.

Settlement of the West

Many explorers, traders, woodsmen, and setters followed in the footsteps of Lewis and Clark. They made the West their home, spreading the American way of life to the Pacific coast. This westward expansion pushed back the frontier, defined a new American border, and made the United States a primary landholder in North America.

Beginning of the End

Within 50 years of the end of the Lewis and Clark Expedition, settlers came to farm the land and a railway was built to the West Coast. The buffalo herds that roamed freely on the Great Plains were nearly wiped out by hunters eager to clear the land for farming. The American Indians who welcomed Lewis and Clark as friends fought European diseases. Eventually, weakened from disease, and hunger from the loss of their main food source, American Indians were forced into government **reservations**. Many did not willingly go, and resisted this change and the loss of their freedom for many years.

(left) Many American Indians do not celebrate the Lewis and Clark Expedition as a great American accomplishment. It permanently changed the way they lived and took away their lands.

30

(background) The journals of the Lewis and Clark Expedition paint a picture of life in the American West 200 years ago. Lewis and Clark and several members of the Corps of Discovery made detailed notes of what they did every day. They made maps, sketched plants, described the weather and even what they ate and how they ate it. These important documents of American history describe the wildlife, plants, and people of the West in the days before European settlers came.

Glossary

calico Cotton cloth that is printed with brightly colored patterns

chronometer A device that keeps very precise time

colony Land ruled by a distant country

confluence The point where two or more streams or rivers flow together

court martial A military court, presided over by officers and following military law

current The direction that the path of moving water in a river follows

dysentery A severe bodily infection that results in violent diarrhea, fever, and pain

governor The person appointed to rule over a territory or colony

Indian Affairs A government department created in 1775 to negotiate treaties with American Indians

interpreter Someone who translates words from one language to another

marksman Someone who is skilled at shooting

militia An army made up of citizens, not professional soldiers

moccasins Soft leather footwear originally made and worn by North American Indians

mouth The part of a stream or river that empties into a larger body of water

planter A plantation owner

plied Sailed over regularly

pole To move a boat forward using one or more long poles

portage To carry boats and supplies overland due to unnavigable water

reservation A tract of land set aside by a government for a specific group of people

Revolutionary War The 1775 to 1783 war between the United States and Britain which resulted in an independent United States of America

stockade A tall wooden barrier

superintendent A person given authority to supervise

trading company A company set up for the purpose of buying and selling goods

wampum Small beads or shells strung together and used as currency by American Indians

Index

1 2 3 4 5 6 7 8 9 0   Printed in the U.S.A.   4 3 2 1 0 9 8 7 6 5